W9-COS-768

Easy-to-Make Puppets

With Step-by-Step Instructions

By Mabel Duch

Illustrated by **Gary Mohrmann**

Publishers   PLAYS, INC.   *Boston*

Copyright © 1993
by Mabel Duch

All rights reserved.

Library of Congress Cataloging-in-Publication Data

Duch, Mabel.
    Easy-to-make puppets : with step-by-step instructions / by Mabel
Duch ; illustrations by Gary Mohrmann.
           p.   cm.
    Summary: Presents instructions and patterns for making nineteen
simple hand, finger, and rod puppets.
    ISBN 0-8238-0300-7
    1. Puppet making--Juvenile literature. [1. Puppet making.
2. Handicraft.] I. Mohrmann, Gary, ill. II. Title.
TT174.7.D83 1993
745.592'24--dc20   93-15320
                                            CIP
                                            AC

Printed in the United States of America

Introduction

Over twenty years of teaching experience has convinced me of the educational value of puppets and puppet making. Children of all ages love puppets and like to make their own. This book lets them do it with a minimum of adult help.

There is a need for inexpensive, easily made, fun-to-use puppets at all grade levels as well as a need for precise, easy-to-follow directions. With this in mind, I'd like to share some of my unique puppets with you.

Each puppet recipe contains a list of materials, step-by-step directions, full-sized patterns where needed, and a picture of the finished product. Older children will be able to make the basic puppets independently, adding creative touches of their own. Younger children can successfully complete the puppets with little help from adults.

Most of the materials can be found in your own home or school. You may need to purchase tongue depressors and pipe cleaners from your drugstore; gummed circles and colored art tape from a stationery or office supply store; craft sticks and colored feathers from a craft store; sponge rubber (polyfoam) from an upholstery or upholstery supply shop, carpet store, or supermarket.

Because many of the puppet recipes are for action and rhythm puppets, music will add to the fun.

The puppets in this book are just a sample of what you can make using common materials. After you have tried the puppets, experiment and see what you and your children can create!

Table of Contents

SINGING BIRD

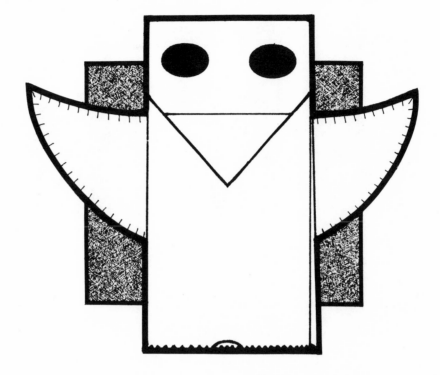

Before he flies to his winter home, Singing Bird would like to visit your classroom and sing with the children.

Materials needed:

a paper sack, 8½ by 5 or 11 by 5½ inches

a piece of light cardboard or yellow construction paper, 9 by 6 inches, for beak

a piece of brown construction paper, 9 by 12 inches or a 9 by 12-inch piece of heavy paper bag for wings

a piece of tracing paper or thin typing paper for tracing wing pattern

a piece of heavy paper, 4 by 6 inches for beak pattern

pencil, scissors, white glue, black marker and yellow marker (if beak material is white)

Lay the sack flat in front of you with the bottom of the sack on top.

Fold under the lower corners and glue. **Do not** fold under the top corners.

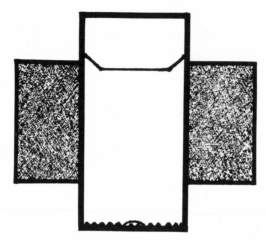

To make Singing Bird's beak:

To make a pattern, fold in half a piece of paper 4 inches long and slightly wider than the lower edge of the bird's face.

Cut diagonally from open edges to folded side. Open up paper and you have a beak pattern.

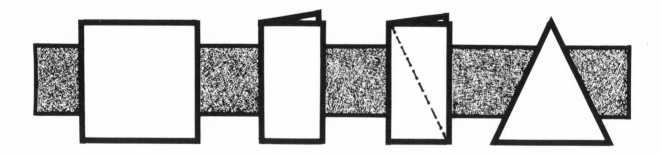

Using pattern, cut two beaks from light cardboard or construction paper. Color yellow, if necessary.

Glue one beak to the underside of the bottom of the face flap. Be sure the base of the beak which shows is exactly as wide as the bottom edge of the face flap.

Glue the other beak on the front of the paper bag. Glue it directly under the top beak so the beak points and edges meet when Singing Bird's mouth is closed.

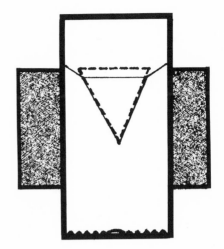

Trace this oval to make a pattern for Singing Bird's eyes.

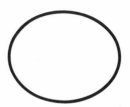

Place the eyes straight across and wide apart (about a half inch from sides of face). The top of each eye should be ¾ inch from the top of the head.

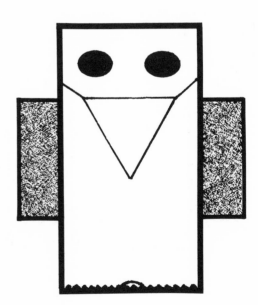

Singing Bird needs one more thing— his wings.

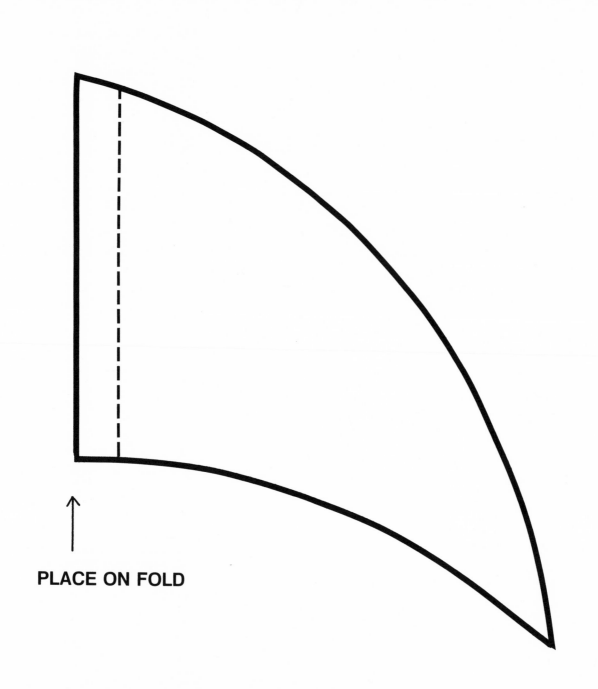

PLACE ON FOLD

Here is the pattern for Singing Bird's wings. Trace and cut out. Place on folded 9 by 12-inch brown construction paper or a folded piece of heavy, brown paper bag. Trace around and cut out.

Fold back wings on dotted lines (about ½ inch from center fold).

Open wings out and put glue on center inch of wings (outlined by folds).

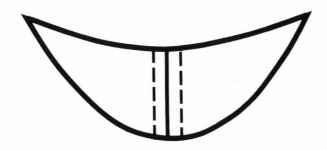

Put one hand inside Singing Bird to keep the glue from soaking through to front. With other hand, press center of wings on center of bird's back. Press firmly and hold a minute.

With scissors, make small cuts on edges of wings to fringe them.

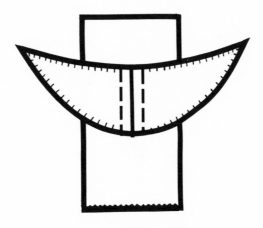

Fold wings back on outside fold lines.

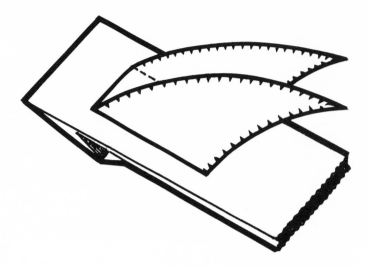

Put your hand inside Singing Bird, palm forward. Bend your fingers and put your fingertips against the base of his beak. Push your fingertips back and forth to make him sing or talk. Your bird's wings will flap slightly as his beak opens and closes. He looks like he's ready to fly.

If you stand behind a prop tree, you can fly Singing Bird from limb to limb.

FEATHER BIRD

A delightfully mobile puppet can be made very simply.

Materials needed:
    a bead of about ½-inch diameter
    a feather about 7 inches long
    a yard of black thread
    a ¼-inch gummed circle* and a little white glue

Put a **little** glue around opening of bead. Push feather through. Tie thread loosely next to bead, on feather side. Push bead and thread back until bead and feather balance. Let glue dry. Tighten thread. Remove any fuzz on ''beak.'' Make two eyes from a gummed circle and stick on two sides of bead.

Cut thread to length which lets you easily handle it. Walk with bird on the end of your thread moving it up and down as you go. Your bird will look like he's flying. Experiment and see what you can make him do.

If you like, tape thread to end of straw. When not in use, wind thread onto straw so it won't tangle.

*available in stationery or office supply stores

TEN LITTLE JACK-O'-LANTERNS

Ten little jack-o'-lanterns, faces all aglow;
One stands up and says, "Let's go!"

Ten little jack-o'-lanterns in a nice straight line;
One topples over; now there are nine.

Nine little jack-o'-lanterns walking out the gate;
One stumbles on a stick; now there are eight.

Eight little jack-o'-lanterns meet a hungry cow;
Cow grabs a mouthful; there's only seven now.

Seven little jack-o'-lanterns thinking up tricks;
One thinks so hard he breaks his head; now there are six.

Six little jack-o'-lanterns breathe like they're alive;
One puffs his light out; now there are five.

Five little jack-o'-lanterns knocking on your door;
One runs and hides; now there are four.

Four little jack-o'-lanterns chuckling happily;
One falls and starts to cry; now there are three.

Three little jack-o'-lanterns say, "How do you do?"
One turns and runs away; now there are two.

Two little jack-o'-lanterns think trick or treating's fun;
One breaks his candy sack; now there's only one.

One lonely jack-o'-lantern. Whatever will he do?
He jumps up on your windowsill and there he shines for you.

TEN LITTLE JACK-O'-LANTERNS FINGER PUPPETS

Materials needed:

a nickel and a penny for patterns

two well-fitting black gloves (leather preferred)

two 6 by 4½-inch pieces of construction paper, one orange and one black

about ten ¾-inch yellow adhesive-backed circles

four or more ¼-inch yellow adhesive-backed circles

black adhesive-backed tape or strapping tape

black fine line marker, black pen, pencil, scissors and glue

Trace a penny ten times on orange paper. Make jack-o'-lantern faces except for eyes. Use ¼-inch circles for eyes or cut from ¾-inch circles. Trace around eyes with black pen. Cut out faces.

Trace a nickel ten times on black construction paper. Cut out. Glue faces to black circles so a little black shows around each face. Let dry.

Place your jack-o'-lanterns right side up, eyes toward top of face. Turn each one over and place a drop of glue or a small roll of tape on back.

Strapping tape will hold jack-o'-lanterns securely, but may show when you duck them down. Black gummed tape (available at stationery and art and craft stores) is not as adhesive, but will not show and will adhere adequately if pressed on firmly.

Put on black gloves. Press each finger down firmly on back of a jack-o'-lantern. If using glue, pull glove away from finger slightly until dry.

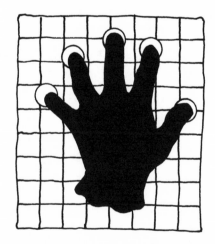

As you do finger play, fold each finger down in turn. Extinguished jack-o'-lanterns should be virtually invisible. One finger should remain as last jack-o'-lantern.

PUMPKIN HEAD

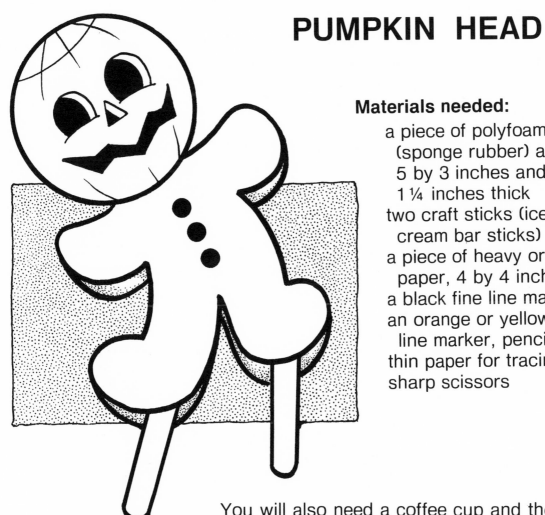

Materials needed:

a piece of polyfoam
  (sponge rubber) at least
  5 by 3 inches and ¾ to
  1 ¼ inches thick
two craft sticks (ice-
  cream bar sticks)
a piece of heavy orange
  paper, 4 by 4 inches
a black fine line marker
an orange or yellow fine
  line marker, pencil, glue
thin paper for tracing
sharp scissors

You will also need a coffee cup and the pattern below.

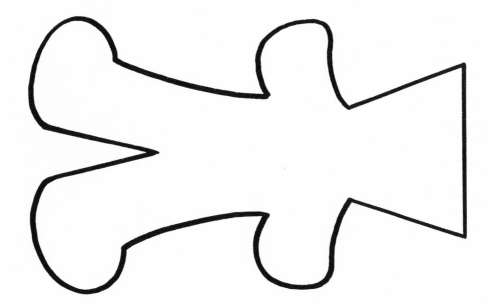

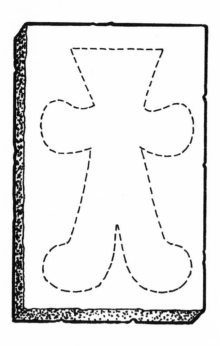

Trace the pattern. Cut your pattern out and place on the sponge. Trace around it with orange or yellow fine line marker.

Cut out your Pumpkin Head's body. Thick sponges will cut easier if you cut with the sponge near the back part of your blades.

To make head, place coffee cup on orange paper; trace around and cut out the circle.

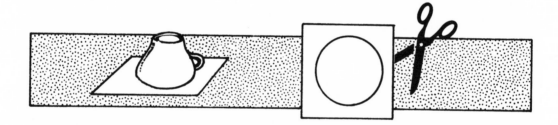

Next, you will make the eyes, nose and mouth of your Pumpkin Head. Here are some patterns you may use. After tracing or drawing them on your circle, fill in features with black marker.

Glue pumpkin head firmly to front of puppet's neck.

Your Pumpkin Head puppet is finished now, except for the sticks which will let him dance.

Push narrow scissor blade into the soles of each of your puppet's feet, near the heels. Push a craft stick into the hole and up into one leg until it is held tightly by sponge. Pull down gently on leg as you push. Repeat for other leg.

You should have almost three inches of stick left for handles.

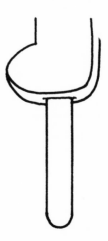

Pumpkin Head is ready for action now. Hold one of his sticks in your right hand and the other in your left. Make him dance by pushing up on the sticks one at a time. Push until his hand almost touches his leg. The faster you push his sticks, the faster he will dance.

Your puppet will bow if you turn his toes to the front. Turn his toes toward each other and he will bow deeper. Play with him and see what else he can do.

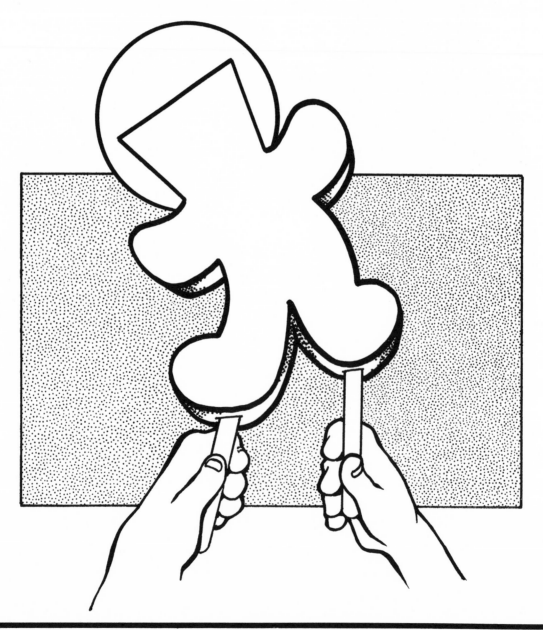

SMALL WITCH

Materials needed:
    a used-up wide water-
      color marker
    black cloth, 14 x 14
      inches
    black paper, 8 x 8
      inches
    white cardboard, 3 by 4
      inches
    scissors, pencil, white
      glue
    black fine line marker
    red fine line marker
    blue, green or brown fine
      line marker
    cellophane tape
    soup spoon (for a pat-
      tern)

To make the dress:

Find the exact center of the cloth by folding left to right and then top to bottom. Press down with hands to make fold marks. Unfold cloth. With pencil or scissor point, poke hole in the center of the cloth.

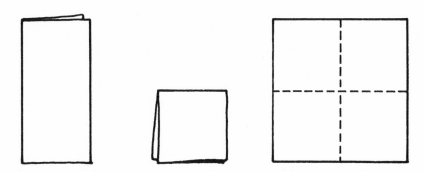

Take cap off marker. Push the felt tip of the marker through the hole in the cloth. Put cap back on, so it holds the cloth tightly.

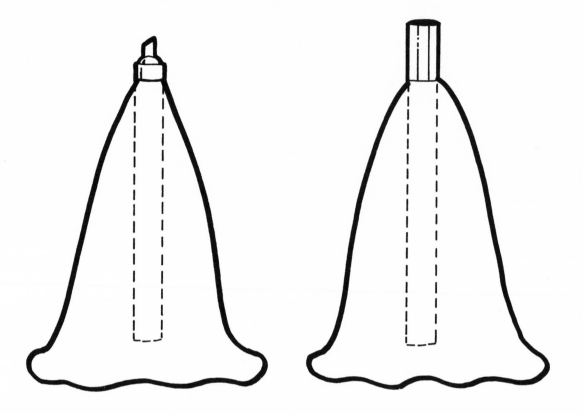

To make the head:

Lay spoon face down on cardboard and trace around bowl of spoon. Cut out and tape head tightly to marker cap.

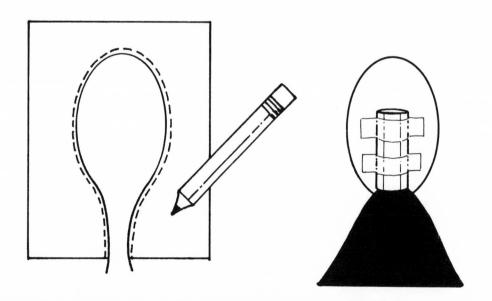

To make curls, cut four strips of black paper, 8 inches long and ½ inch wide. Run strips between scissor blade and thumb to curl. Fold uncurled ends over front of head and tape down. Tape to back of head, too.

To make the hat:

Trace the triangle pattern and cut out. Place your pattern on black paper and cut two copies. Fold up bottom edge of each piece ¼ inch. Glue one piece to back of Small Witch's head with folded-up brim resting on marker cap. Glue the other piece of hat to the front of Small Witch's head and to the other hat half.

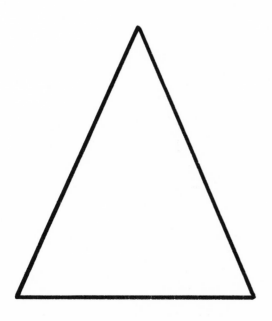

Cut off the corners of the brim of the back half so it makes a smooth line with the edge of the front brim.

With fine line markers, draw Small Witch's eyes, mouth, nose and eyebrows.

Hold her body firmly with three fingers and extend your thumb and forefinger to the front.

At the points where your finger and thumb push out Small Witch's dress, make small cuts just big enough for your thumb and forefinger to poke through and act as the little witch's arms. She can clap her hands, scratch her chin, wave and hold things.

If you roll the marker back and forth in your hand, Small Witch will shake her head from side to side.

You can make other marker puppets. Just omit hat, add more curls and glue them to head.

QUICK SPOON PUPPET

Materials needed:

    a plastic teaspoon
    one square foot of thin to
      medium cloth
    about six pieces of
      4-inch yarn tied in the
      middle with another
      piece
    about two inches of
      ¾-inch colored art
      tape
    small piece of black tape
    two ¼-inch gummed
      circles (green, blue or
      brown)
    one red ¼-inch gummed
      circle
    (Small bits of colored
      paper can be used in-
      stead.)
    scissors and white glue

Cut a small hole in center of cloth. (See ''Small Witch'' for method of finding center.) Push spoon handle through and tape cloth dress to puppet's neck. Rounded (convex) part of spoon is face. If you like, cut holes for finger arms. (See ''Small Witch.'')

Apply from ½ to ¾ of red circle for mouth. Use other circles for eyes. Cut slim ends off black tape for eyebrows (or cut features from colored paper and glue to face). Glue tied yarn to face of spoon at the **top**. Hold until partly dry. Let dry completely before using puppet.

You can get a surprising amount of action from little ''Spoon Puppet'' by shaking and twisting her in your hand.

STICK PUPPET TURKEY
(nonedible)

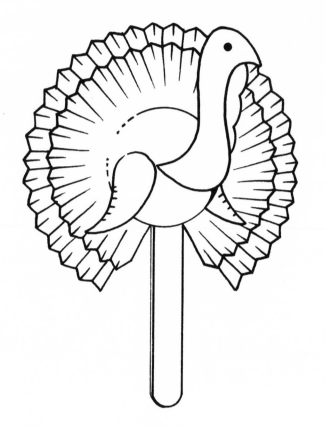

Materials needed:

a tongue depressor
1 by 1-foot piece of
 stiff brown paper (a
 grocery sack is fine)
4 by 8 inches of thin
 brown paper (small
 sack)
a 2 by 3-inch piece of
 red paper or 5 inches
 of ¾-inch red art
 tape
one egg section from
 an egg carton
black and brown fine
 line markers
white glue
thin, white paper for
 tracing
pencil and these pat-
 terns

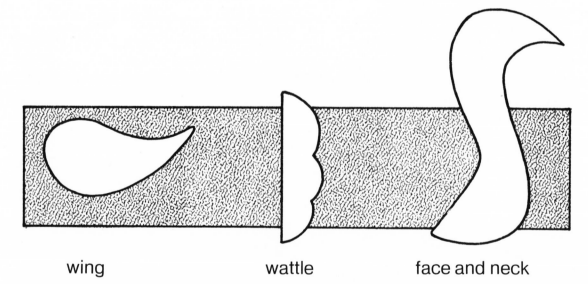

wing   wattle   face and neck

Cut a 5-inch circle and a 4-inch circle from stiff paper. Cut a pie serving section out of each. Scallop edges or trace these patterns to use.

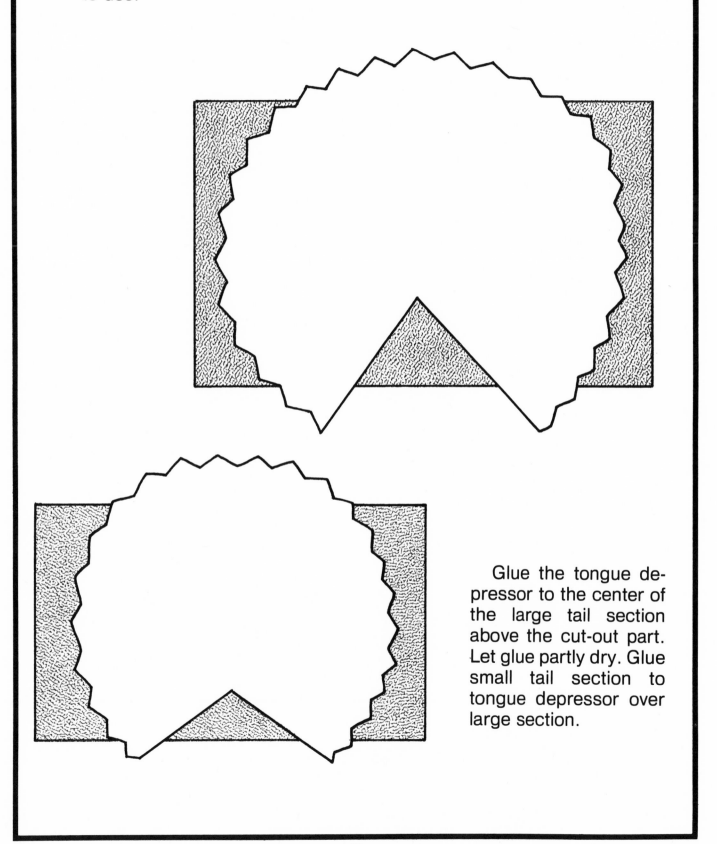

Glue the tongue depressor to the center of the large tail section above the cut-out part. Let glue partly dry. Glue small tail section to tongue depressor over large section.

Trim egg carton section so it will lie flat. Glue to center of tail.

Cut thin paper into eleven 4-inch-long narrow strips (no wider than ¼ inch). Glue criss-cross over egg carton section and to tail. Try not to glue any to stick. When finished, glue one strip around bottom of egg carton section, over crossed ends.

Trace and use your head and wattle patterns. Cut two heads from stiff brown paper. Cut two wattles from red paper or tape. Glue (or stick) the two wattles together.

Glue wattle to one head and neck piece with largest part of it under turkey's chin.

Fold back pointed parts of turkey's neck so they rest flat on center of egg section body. Glue rest of head halves together. Glue pointed parts to body.

When glue is dry, make black eyes. With brown marker, draw lines between and on tail feathers.

If you want wings, use the wing pattern. Make feather marks on concave curve. Glue rounded part of wing to body.

Now your turkey is ready to gobble and strut. Turn him from side to side slightly so his handsome head can be seen.

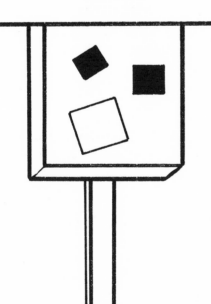

GEOMETRIC RHYTHM DANCERS

Materials needed:

a box 4 to 6 inches tall, 1 ¾ to 2½ inches wide and ¾ to 2½ inches deep*

a 6 by 6-inch piece of light to medium weight cardboard (tagboard or poster board in pretty colors)

geometric figures (squares, circles, triangles or rectangles) cut from construction paper, or adhesive-backed geometric labels from an office supply or stationery store

a black fine line marker

a craft stick

nylon strapping tape

cellophane tape

glue, if needed

something to rattle (beads, beans, rice, seeds or a jingle bell)

a feather or feathers and construction paper to cover box, if desired (about 6 by 18 inches)

*Boxes from mounted slides are excellent.

Put rattle material inside box. Tape box closed with strapping tape. Then tape craft stick securely to back of box.

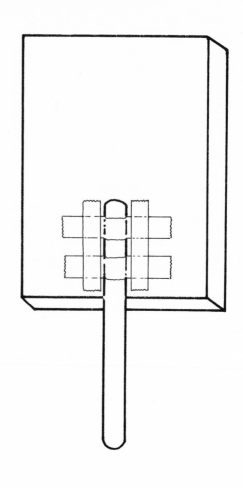

Cover box with construction paper, if you like. Many boxes will be attractive enough so this will not be necessary. Do **not** cover bottom.

Cut a 4 by 4-inch square from cardboard. Make and attach features. Use glue, if needed.

(Suggested feature sizes: mouth—1-inch square; eyes—¾-inch squares; pupils—¼-inch squares; eyebrows and nose—small squares made with black fine line marker.)

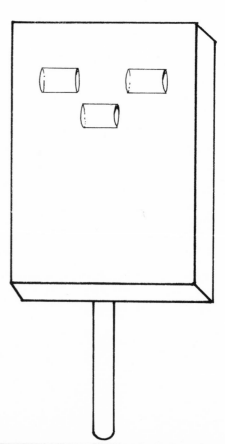

Attach feather or feathers to back of head with cellophane tape.

Place strapping tape rolls or glue on front of box above midline. Place head over this area. Push down to stick.

Stand your Square Dancer on the edge of a table or desk while you work on more dancers.

To make **Circle Dancer**, use a lid from a small (8 ounce) margarine tub as a head pattern.

Eyes and mouth are halves of 1¼-inch circles or whole 1-inch circles. Make nose and curved eyebrows with black marker.

Rectangle Dancer's head is 5 by 4 inches. His mouth is about 1 by ½ inch. His nose is a ½ to ¾-inch square. (Remember squares are rectangles.) Pupils are ¼ to 3/8-inch squares. Whiskers and forehead line are long narrow rectangles.

To make **Triangle Dancer** cut a triangle with 5½ to 6-inch sides. Use triangles with 1-inch base for eyes, ¾-inch base triangle for mouth and a smaller one for nose. Narrow triangles make the eyebrows.

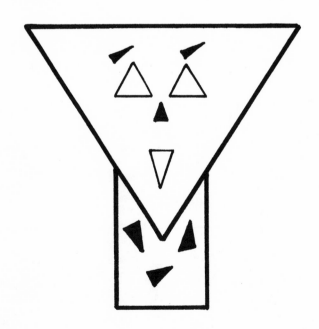

Make some drums by covering cylindrical oatmeal boxes or coffee cans with paper. Decorate with markers, paint or paper strips.

Beat a rhythm on a drum while the Geometric Rhythm Dancers hop up and down in time to the beat; hop to the right; hop to the left; tip forward to bow.

Note to parents and teachers: To reinforce left to right progression, show children how to dance puppets from **their** left to **their** right along the edge of a stage (screen or table). A feather attached to the right side of a puppet's head, as a puppeteer sees it, will help establish sense of direction. Let children practice, taking turns with drums and puppets.

Teach them how to "read" a simple rhythm. Use dots to represent soft beats, lines to represent hard or accented beats. (Example: __ . __ . __ . __ .) Have children practice increasingly complex rhythm patterns with their drums and puppets. Let them write some, too.

RHYTHM REINDEER

The Rhythm Reindeer is made like the Geometric Rhythm Dancers, with a jingle bell inside.

Materials needed:

9 by 6 inches of brown paper to cover body (a cut paper sack is fine)

6 by 6 inches of stiff brown paper (heavy sack) for antlers

6 by 6 inches of brown cardboard for head (a light shade is best) and a medium brown marker

3 by 3 inches of black paper, about 6 inches of ¾-inch black, gummed art tape, or a fine black marker; a 1-inch square of red paper, a red marker or an inch of red, gummed tape (if you want a red-nosed reindeer, you will need ¾ by 2 inches of red), a sheet of thin paper for tracing and a pencil; glue (if needed) and a box, stick and tape as detailed in ''Geometric Rhythm Dancers.''

To make body, follow directions for Geometric puppets.

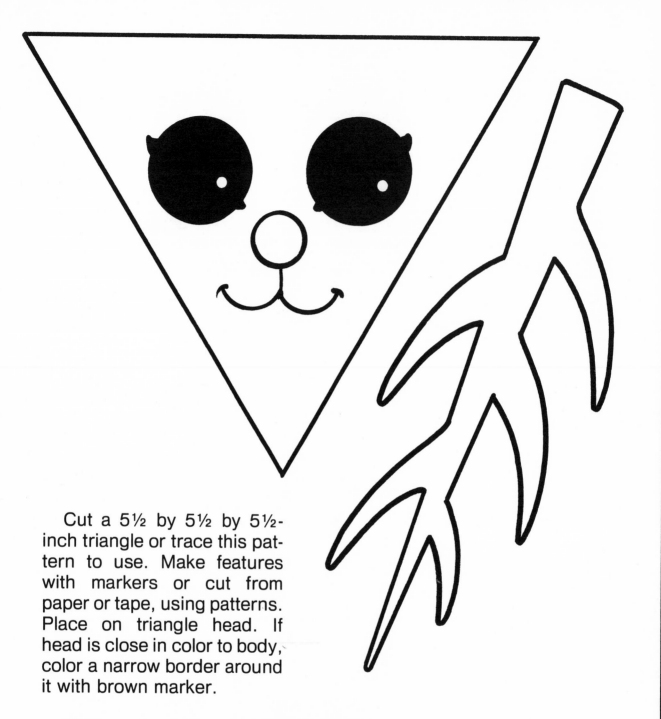

Cut a 5½ by 5½ by 5½-inch triangle or trace this pattern to use. Make features with markers or cut from paper or tape, using patterns. Place on triangle head. If head is close in color to body, color a narrow border around it with brown marker.

Trace, cut and use antler pattern. (The pattern is for the reindeer's left antler. Reverse for right.) Tape antlers to back of head. Strengthen with strip of cellophane tape.

Fasten head to body with two rolls of strapping tape. Your reindeer is now ready for a jingle bell dance or a play.

INSTANT SANTAS

Materials needed:

    Old Christmas cards and/or Christmas wrapping paper with
      Santas on them

    thin cardboard (about the heaviness of good file cards or file
      folders)

    thin paste (¼ cup flour, 2 tablespoons sugar, ¼ cup water;
      mix sugar and flour, gradually add water, stirring until
      smooth, store in tightly covered jar)

    scissors

    coffee stirrers and/or red and white plastic drinking straws

To make Christmas card Santas:

Cut out Santas from cards. Tape coffee stirrers or straws to backs of Santas. (For thin cards, see below.)

To make wrapping paper Santas:

Rough cut Santas from wrapping paper. Spread paste evenly on back. Paste to thin cardboard. Let dry **thoroughly**.

Cut out Santas as neatly as you can, cutting through excess paper and cardboard. Tape coffee stirrer or straw to back of Santa and he's ready for action.

If you can find Santas engaged in various activities, you can incorporate these into your Santa plays (for example: making toys, packing his bag, carrying bag).

Also look for reindeer, elves, snowmen, Christmas trees and other interesting characters on cards and wrapping paper.

TOY SOLDIER

Materials needed:

a cardboard tube about 3½ inches long and 1½ inches in diameter (from tube of bathroom tissue roll or cut from paper towel core)

one craft (ice-cream bar) stick

smooth white or tan paper, 3½ by 7 inches

black construction paper, 4 by 9 inches

a small bright piece of adhesive-backed paper or construction paper and glue

a black and a red fine line marker

a larger red marker (or red paint and brush)

pencil and scissors

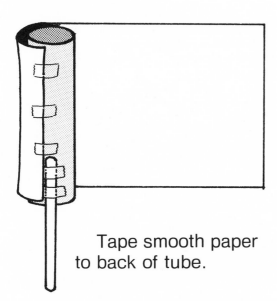

Tape smooth paper to back of tube.

Tape craft stick to outside of cardboard tube, so there are three inches of stick below the tube, for the soldier's handle.

Wrap tightly around tube. Tape end of paper down lengthwise, with about 1½ inches of extra tape at each end. Stick the extra tape to the inside of the tube so the paper will be held firmly to the tube.

With black fine line marker, draw eyes, eyebrows and nose. Make a mouth with red fine line marker.

With a pencil, sketch uniform, arms, sash and shoes on paper-covered tube. Leave sash and arms uncolored. Color or paint the rest of the uniform red. Make the shoes black. Draw a fine red line between top of sash and face. With red fine line marker, decorate arms like picture.

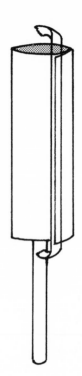

To strengthen holding stick, fasten to body with a small piece of tape from stick to outside of body.

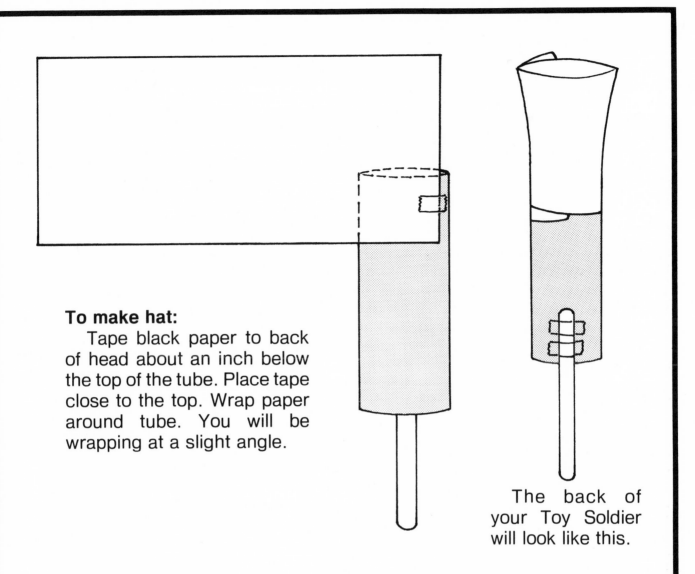

To make hat:

Tape black paper to back of head about an inch below the top of the tube. Place tape close to the top. Wrap paper around tube. You will be wrapping at a slight angle.

The back of your Toy Soldier will look like this.

Fasten front of hat with flower or decoration cut from adhesive-backed paper. Or glue together and cover with paper flower or decoration.

Flatten the hat slightly at the top so it will be wider. Trim hat so it is even across the top. Fasten to body with tape in back.

Now your soldier is ready to march.

MITTEN DOLL

Materials needed:

    one pretty mitten
    piece of 4 by 4-inch light
      cardboard
    black fine point marker
    paint
    paper towel tubing
    bright construction
      paper
    scissors and glue or
      tape

Using a cup or glass as a pattern, trace and cut a cardboard circle slightly smaller than the finger section of your mitten.

With a black fine point marker, outline eyes and make eyebrows and eyelashes. Paint a mouth, or draw one with red marker.

Glue or tape face to mitten.

34

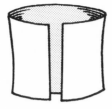 

To make skirt:

Cut two 1½-inch pieces from a paper towel tube. Make a lengthwise cut in each paper towel tube section.

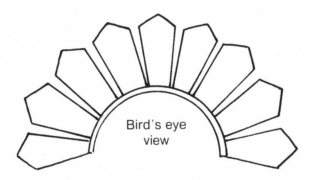

Bird's eye view

Cut bright paper into two 3 by 6-inch pieces. Cover tube pieces with paper, gluing ½ inch to inside of one end of each tube.

Paper will extend about one inch beyond the opposite ends. Fold this one inch of paper back and cut into points.

To try on paper skirt, put mitten on your hand. Put one skirt section on the back of your wrist, one on the front.

(Another skirt effect can be achieved by sewing a pretty ribbon to your Mitten Doll's waist.)

Mitten puppets can bend and turn and twist, bow and wave. They are as flexible and as active as your hand.

Variations are endless.

What might you devise?

DANCING VALENTINE

Materials needed:

    a polyfoam sponge, 5½ by 4 inches and 1 to 1½ inches thick

    two jumbo size plastic straws

    a 4 by 4-inch piece of white lightweight cardboard or pink construction paper

    a black fine line marker and a red one

    sharp scissors and glue

    pencil and thin paper for tracing

Here is a pattern you may trace for making Dancing Valentine's body. Be careful not to make legs any thinner than pattern's legs.

Follow the directions for Pumpkin Head's body, except for the feet.

With scissors, cut a small X on each foot, directly under the leg. Push scissor point in about ¾ of an inch. Turn slightly and remove.

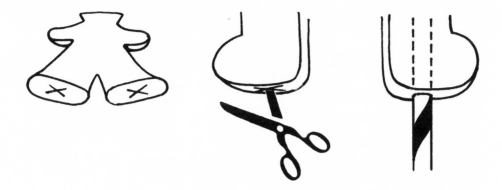

Dip one end of straw in glue. Using the hole the scissors made, push straw into leg. Push beyond where the scissors went, until the straw is held tight by the sponge (about 1½ inches). Repeat with other leg.

Trace Dancing Valentine's head for a pattern. Cut out and trace on cardboard or pink construction paper. Make eyes with black marker, mouth with red and nose with black. Cut out head and glue firmly to neck. Use plenty of glue and hold until partly dry.

If you let the glue in Dancing Valentine's legs dry overnight, he'll be ready for hours and hours of dancing. Cut off a little from the ends of the straws to make them easier to handle. To make your puppet dance, push up and down alternately on his straws.

TEN LITTLE PIGLETS

Ten little piglets dancing in a line;
One hurts his little hoof; now there are nine.

Nine curly tails—no! one's straight;
Leaves to get a tail curl; now there are eight.

Eight little piglets twist and turn and bow;
One topples over; there are only seven now.

Seven little piglets doing circus tricks;
One falls and bumps his head; now there are six.

Six little piglets jump and jig and jive;
One hurts his back; now there are five.

Five little piglets squeezing through the door;
One gets stuck; now there are four.

Four little piglets singing ''Wee, wee, wee'';
One gets a sore throat; now there are three.

Three little piglets wondering what to do;
One falls asleep; now there are two.

Two little piglets lying in the sun;
One gets a sunburn; now there's only one.

One little piglet—she thinks eating's fun;
Soon becomes a big fat hog; now my tale is done.

TEN LITTLE PIGLETS
FINGER PUPPETS

Materials needed:

a penny, a nickel and a fifty cent piece for patterns;
6 by 9 inches of pink and 6 by 4½ inches of black construction paper
one tongue depressor
strapping tape; transparent tape; pencil and scissors
black fine line marker or pen
thin typing paper and carbon paper (optional)

Trace fifty cent piece on pink paper. Trace nickel ten times. Leave some room between circles. Add piggy ears and draw eyes, snout and mouth with fine line marker or pen. Cut pig faces out and put a roll of tape on the back of each.

Cover tongue depressor with pink paper. Stick large pig head onto depressor near top.

Trace penny ten times on black paper. Cut each black circle in a spiral. Cut one straight tail.

Pull ends of spiral tails so spiral will open up. With transparent tape, fasten tails to nail side of your fingers. (If you prefer, you may wear pink, white or beige gloves.) Tape one tail to back of tongue depressor pig.

Arrange little piglet faces tape side up with ears toward the top. Press each of your fingers down firmly on tape rolls.

Your piglets are ready to perform. On verse two, turn the backs of your hands to your audience so they can see the piglets' tails.

Have last little pig disappear. Then show large tongue depressor "hog" ("soon becomes a big fat hog"). Have "hog" turn around and disappear ("now my tale is done").

BUNNY PUPPET

Materials needed:

    half an insulated (styrofoam)
      cup, cut lengthwise
    a white file card
    a craft (ice-cream bar) stick
    a cotton ball
    a red pen
    a black pen
    a pink marker
    a piece of thin typing paper
    a pencil, glue and cello-
      phane tape.

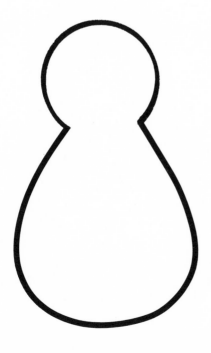

Trace and cut out this bunny pattern. Hold your pattern on the half cup with the bunny's body toward the bottom and the head toward the top. Trace around your bunny pattern with a pencil.

43

DO NOT cut off the bottom of your half cup but cut out the bunny's head and body in one piece, leaving the bottom of the half cup attached to the bottom of the bunny.

Starting at the bottom of the bunny, trim the bottom of the cup so the back of the bottom is no wider than the bottom of the bunny.

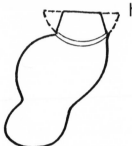

Trim here.

To make ears:

Trace ear pattern. Cut out your pattern. Trace two ears on the file card. Color the middle of the ears pink. Tape Bunny's ears to the back of his head with the pink in front.

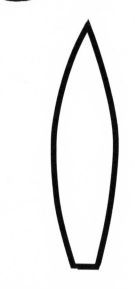

Make bunny's eyes with a red pen. With a black pen, make his mouth, whiskers and paws.

With scissors, make a small slit in the middle of the base (what's left of the bottom of the styrofoam cup). Make a slit parallel to the front of the bunny. This should be just big enough to push the craft stick into it.

Push craft stick up through the slit until its top is about ¾ of an inch above the base.

Glue cotton tail to back of stick so that when the bunny is turned slightly to the side, you can see his tail. The tail should come above and slightly over the top of the stick so you cannot easily see the stick.

You may want to fluff up tail slightly.

Hold bottom of craft stick and hop bunny up and down as you move him back and forth.

He can stand by himself on the edge of a box or other flat surface when not hopping around.

TEN LITTLE BIRDS

Ten little birds on a telephone line;
One gets a call; now there are nine.

Nine little birds staying up late;
One falls asleep; now there are eight;

Eight little birds flying close to heaven;
One flies too high; now there are seven.

Seven little birds do loop-de-loop tricks;
One gets dizzy; now there are six.

Six little birds circle, dip and dive;
One dives too close to earth; now there are five.

Five little birds dip and dive some more;
One gets oh, so tired; now there are four.

Four little birds flying to a tree;
One bumps his head; now there are three.

Three little birds hear ''Tu-whit tu-whoo'';
Owl scares one away; now there are two.

Two little birds decide to build a nest;
What happens next? I think you've guessed.

EASY FINGER PUPPET: BIRD

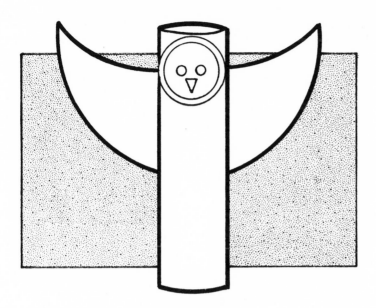

Materials needed:

    cover tube from lipstick (or similar cosmetic) 1 ¼ to 2 ¼ inches long

    piece of Con-Tact paper 4 inches long (should be as wide as length of tube) (some tubes may not need covering)

    small piece of same color Con-Tact paper about 1 ½ by 1 ½ inches (or a circle 1 ½ inches in diameter)

    small piece of yellow paper ½ by ½ inch

    small pieces of colored paper, a little smaller than button

    glue and cellophane tape

    wings:

    colored file card or light cardboard (3 by 5 inches) or two pieces of Con-Tact paper (2 ½ by 2 ½ inches), different color or pattern than Bird's body

Place top of tube in center of 1½ by 1-inch piece of Con-Tact paper. Make 6 to 8 cuts from edge of paper to tube.

Push cut edges against tube, overlapping so they will fit smoothly.

Cover tube with largest piece of Con-Tact paper.

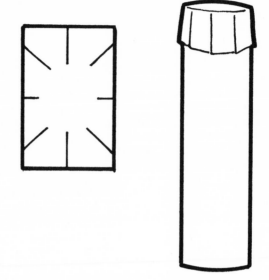

Glue small piece of colored paper to flatter side of button, covering holes.

Cut small yellow paper into triangular beak. Glue to button front.

Glue button to tube just below top.

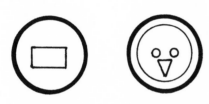

To make wings:

Trace this pattern onto cardboard or back to back on Con-Tact paper and cut out.

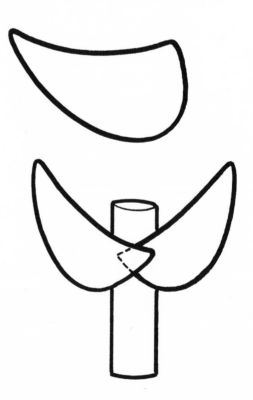

Tape wings to back of bird, overlapping bottom tips slightly. Put him on your finger to fly.

48

Because "Ten Little Birds" is an active finger play, you will need to practice to make it effective. If you do not have a suitable puppet stage, perform from behind a covered table or a large box. Wear long smooth fitting gloves similar in color to your background.

As each bird is eliminated, briefly duck birds out of sight. Place bird between base of two fingers of opposite hand and pull off. Continue to talk, slowly saying, "And then there were . . . ." Pause to give children a chance to say correct number. When they (or you if they don't) say correct number, pop birds up.

Have birds on your two index fingers be remaining two birds. Have them "talk" together on "decide to build a nest." At conclusion, have them fly off together.

Alternate plan: Have five children do play with a bird on each index finger. Size their puppets with paper strips (as wide as the length of the tube and about three inches long). Roll around their fingers, as shown, and insert in tubes. Tape seam and tape to outside. Repeat if necessary.

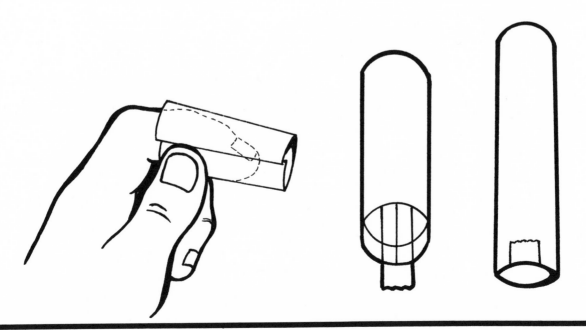

SOME SNIPPETS
(Mini Mike and Friends)

These active little puppets can be made from pieces of fine textured sponge rubber about ½ inch thick.

Besides your sponge rubber and the patterns, you will need:
    pieces of brown or white
      lightweight cardboard about
      1 ¾ by 1 ¾ inches
    a piece of cardboard 3 ¼ by 1 ¾ inches for Bouncy Bunny
    coins (nickel, dime, quarter, fifty cent piece) for head patterns
    a pencil, sharp scissors and fine line felt tip markers
    round toothpicks and strong, white glue
    a cotton ball for Bouncy Bunny

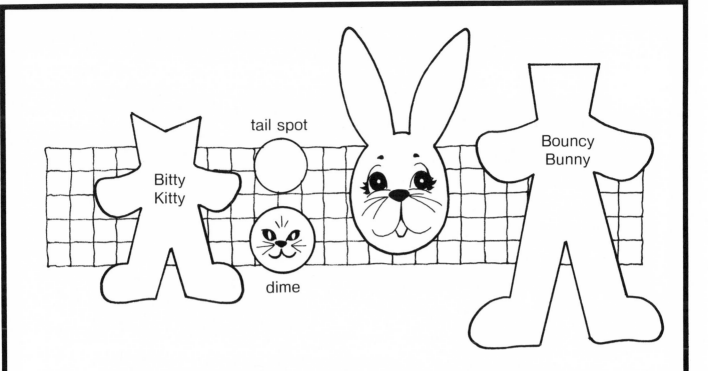

Choose the pattern you need. Lay it on your sponge.

Hold it in place with one hand and trace around it with a light colored marker. (Store pattern in envelope for future use.) Starting with the feet and working upward, cut out your puppet.

With the thicker sponges you may find it easier to cut with the back part of your scissors rather than the points. Place your coin or head pattern on the cardboard and trace around it with your pencil.

You can use the bunny body pattern for a Mini Monster. Use this pattern and a quarter or fifty cent piece to make head.

Glue tail spot to bunny and let dry before gluing on tail.

Color eyes, nose, mouth and hair with your markers. Cut out head and, using plenty of glue, stick it to front of puppet's neck. Hold it in place until it is stuck tightly and glue is partly dry.

Push toothpicks up through the bottom of puppet's feet into legs. Push until toothpicks are held firmly in place.

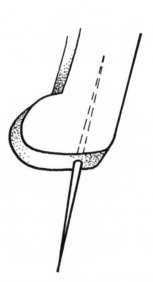

(If the toothpicks are not held tightly by the sponge, pull them out. Dip the tips in glue and push them back in. Do not use puppets for two hours.)

About half of each toothpick should be sticking out of the puppet's feet. Use the toothpicks as handles to make him walk and dance. Push up and down on them one at a time.

Your puppet should bend easily from side to side (far enough to touch his feet or legs). If he does not, take your thumb and forefinger and break off the tip of the toothpick **inside** each leg.

To make each puppet walk, push each toothpick up and over in the direction you want him to move.

These puppets like to dance to music, the peppier, the better. The faster you push up and down, the faster your puppet will dance.

Make puppet bow by pointing toes toward each other.

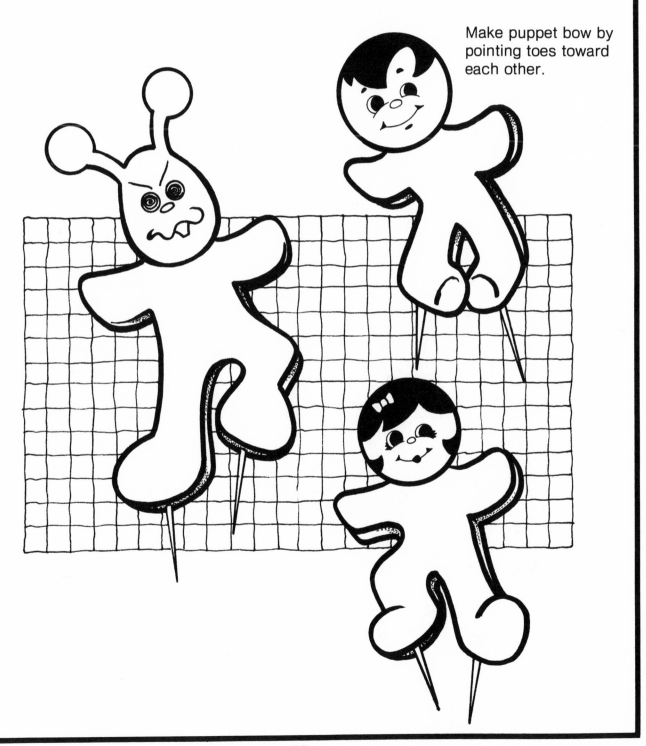

SEE CREATURE

Materials needed:

    50 feet of 4-ply yarn in a
      variegated color
    3 by 5-inch cardboard
    two bright buttons about 5/8
      inches across
    2 inches black art tape
    strong white glue and either
      a yard of black thread or
      an old glove

Cut a 9-inch piece off end of yarn. Wrap the rest around width of cardboard. Pull cut piece between yarn and cardboard. Slip yarn off and tie loops together and tie **tightly** with cut (9-inch) piece.

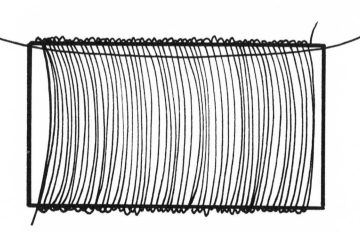

Unravel all yarn. If necessary, trim to achieve round shape. Glue button eyes on your See Creature. If you like, make center of eyes black with shiny black ''art'' tape. Tie to dangle on the end of the thread or glue to back of glove. Put hand in glove and wiggle fingers to make See Creature ''live.''

TEN LITTLE CATERPILLARS

Ten little caterpillars climbing on a vine;
One climbed too high; then there were nine.

Nine little caterpillars crawled out the garden gate;
One got stuck, and then there were eight.

Eight little caterpillars crawled back in again;
One bumped his head; then there were seven.

Seven little caterpillars humped across some sticks;
One got scratched; then there were six.

Six little caterpillars eat to stay alive;
One wiggled away; then there were five.

Five little caterpillars eating more and more;
One got a tummyache; then there were four.

Four little caterpillars climbing up a tree;
One tumbled down; then there were three.

Three little caterpillars wondering what to do;
Along came a bird; then there were two.

Two little caterpillars resting in the sun;
One curled up in a leaf; then there was one.

One little caterpillar resting all alone;
One day became a butterfly; now she has flown.

CATERPILLARS

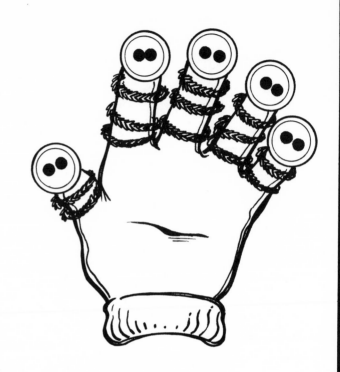

Materials needed:
    a pair of black or brown
      cloth or knit gloves
    ten brightly colored pipe
      cleaners
    ten buttons (about ¾ inch)
      for faces—use brown for
      black gloves, black for
      brown gloves
    twenty ¼-inch dots for eyes
      (any bright color)

Wearing one glove, coil pipe cleaners around each finger. Extend coil beyond end of finger to make caterpillar wiggly and to free fingertips for pulling on and off gloves.

Secure with needle and thread.

Bend over end of each pipe cleaner to make bigger surface. Place button on end. Bend pipe cleaner so button face can be seen when fingers are upright and extended forward.

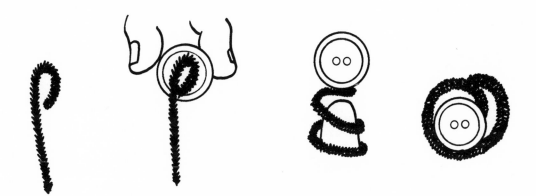

Repeat with other glove.

Place dot eyes over button holes. Glue buttons in place. Let dry.

BUTTERFLY

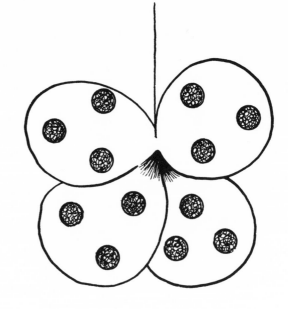

To make butterfly:

Fold fabric square twice, making a smaller square. Cut small square as shown in illustration.

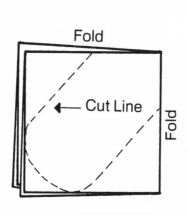

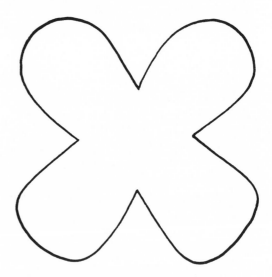

Open cut figure.

Form butterfly's body by gathering center of form between your fingers.

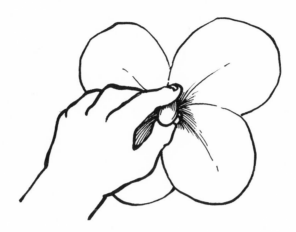

Wrap one end of thread three times around place where body joins wings. Tie. Thread other end on needle. Push needle up through exact center of wings, pulling thread through.

Bend wings to balance, if necessary.

USING CATERPILLARS AND BUTTERFLY

Extend fingers forward and wiggle them as you say the lines to "Ten Little Caterpillars." Fold one finger down for each caterpillar that drops out. It might be easier to make caterpillars disappear one at a time if you perform from behind a box or table.

Hold butterfly by end of thread. Fly by fluttering it up and down and back and forth.

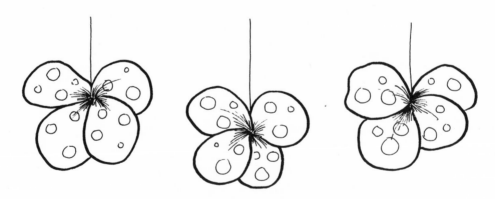

After the one butterfly flies, have it joined by others, if you wish.